I0144113

INSTITUTE OF GENERAL SEMANTICS

# A CONTINUING EDUCATION GUIDE TO TEACHING

## *General Semantics*

### Martin H. Levinson, PhD

Copyright © 2014 by Martin H. Levinson

All rights reserved. No parts of this book may be reproduced, stored in a retrieval system or transmitted in any form or by any means without the prior written permission of the publisher.

First printing

Cover & Interior Book Design by Scribe Freelance

ISBN: 978-0-9860764-9-7

## Other titles included in
## The *New Non-Aristotelian Library* Series
### *Corey Anton, Series Editor*

Korzybski, Alfred  (2010).  *Selections from Science and Sanity*. 2nd Ed.  Edited by Lance Strate, with a Foreword by Bruce I. Kodish.  Fort Worth, TX: Institute of General Semantics.

Strate, Lance  (2011).  *On the Binding Biases of Time and Other Essays on General Semantics and Media Ecology*.  Fort Worth, TX: Institute of General Semantics.

Anton, Corey  (2011). *Communication Uncovered: General Semantics and Media Ecology*.  Fort Worth, TX: Institute of General Semantics.

Levinson, Martin H.  (2012).  *More Sensible Thinking*. New York, NY: Institute of General Semantics.

Anton, Corey & Strate, Lance  (2012).  *Korzybski And* . . .  (Eds.) New York, NY: Institute of General Semantics.

# Table of Contents

# General Semantics

## *A Brief Overview*

### Martin H. Levinson, PhD

General semantics (GS) is a process-oriented, problem-solving system that trains individuals to make their language and thinking more relative to objective reality in order to better evaluate and understand the world. It was originally formulated by Alfred Korzybski, a Polish engineer and intellectual who came to the United States during World War I.

Korzybski was dismayed by the massive carnage and destruction that he observed during the Great War, a feeling that led him to examine the question of why humans haven't made the same progress in dealing with each other as they have in science and technology. From his ten-year-plus study of that question he formulated general semantics, more fully presented in his magnum opus *Science and Sanity: An Introduction to Non-Aristotelian Systems and General Semantics.*

The word "general" precedes "semantics" in order to avoid the traditional philosophic connotations of the term *semantics* and to include portions of Korzybski's general theory of time-binding. Humans are time-binders because they can communicate abstract information not only immediately and directly but also in recorded form; we can write, videotape, voice-record, etc. Each generation inherits the accumulated knowledge of the preceding generation and builds upon it. The focus of GS has been on the development of techniques to make people more effective time-binders.

From the beginning, Korzybski and his students considered GS a practical discipline, to be used by individuals, groups, and organizations to solve problems and make productive decisions. The first two popular books on the subject—*The Tyranny of Words* by Stuart Chase and *Language in Action* by S. I. Hayakawa (later titled *Language in Thought and Action*)—reflected the pragmatic approach, as each author used GS to examine and assess the influence of language on thought and behavior. Subsequent individuals have employed GS to analyze and work out problems in a wide variety of fields such as education, communication, negotiation, management, social science, journalism, and personal adjustment.[1]

Many thinkers, educators, therapists, and other professionals have contributed to the system and GS ideas and formulations have been taught in numerous college courses throughout the world. Over the years, many articles on the benefits of GS have appeared in the *General Semantics Bulletin* and *ETC: A Review of General Semantics* and more than 150 doctoral and master's degree theses have demonstrated its efficacy. General semantics is clearly a highly useful methodology with a wide range of applicability in diverse areas of human endeavor.

## The Lessons

This guide contains twelve continuing education lessons in general semantics.[2] Each lesson includes an *Introduction* (for the teacher) of the basic GS ideas to be presented, a *Motivation* to begin the lesson, and *Suggested Activities* for students. Information from books listed in the *Annotated GS Bibliography* can be used to supplement the instruction, as can info from the GS Learning Center, which can be accessed online at: www.generalsemantics.org/the-general-semantics-learning-center/teaching-materials.

Words printed in Rockwell font (such as this phrase contained within the parentheses) denote teacher comments that can be read or paraphrased. Homework assignments can be reviewed each week or whenever the teacher deems appropriate. Lessons can be combined or abbreviated depending on the time constraints of the course and wishes of the instructor.

# Lesson 1:
## *Science-Related Ideas for Effective Communication and Problem Solving*

Dogma says: "This is so."

Fiction says: "This isn't so, but let's pretend that it is."

A scientific hypothesis says: "Perhaps this is so; let's see if it is."

—Kenneth G. Johnson, *General Semantics: An Outline Survey*

## Introduction

Irving J. Lee, a GS expert and author of the book *Language Habits In Human Affairs,* notes, "Language plays a tremendous role in human affairs. It serves as a means of cooperation and as a weapon of conflict. With it, men can solve problems, erect the towering structures of science and poetry—and talk themselves into insanity and social confusion."[3] General semantics is particularly concerned with the relationship of language and human behavior and how we understand the world.

This lesson seeks to have students discover how words influence thoughts, actions, and emotions. It aims to show how the scientific method and operational definitions are useful ways to facilitate effective problem solving and human communication. It emphasizes the notion that strictly speaking, words don't "mean," people do.

## Motivation

Ask the students to write down their definitions for each of the following terms and have some of them read those definitions to the group.

happiness

success

failure

freedom

intelligence

Note that everyone did not come up with the same definitions. That's because strictly speaking, *words* don't "mean," *people* do. The physicist P. W. Bridgman put it this way, "Never ask 'What does word X mean?' but ask instead, 'What do I mean when I say word X?' or, 'What do you mean when you say word X?' "[4] Words do not have one true meaning. Professor Kenneth Johnson, in his guide *General Semantics: An Outline Survey*, points out that for the 500 most used words in the English language, the *Oxford Dictionary* lists 14,070 meanings.[5]

Words mean different things to different people. The field of contract law is based on this principle.

Words mean different things at different times. In 1896, nine men on the U.S. Supreme Court said that separate but equal facilities for blacks and whites are constitutional. In 1954, nine different men said, in effect, that *separate* and *equal* are opposites.

And words mean different things in different contexts. For example: He *beat* the drum with a stick. *Beats* me. The reporter has the mayor on his *beat*. He *beat* Joe at chess.

Since words and their meanings can be elusive, one way to view communication is as a game in which the speaker and listener (writer and reader) battle against the forces of confusion. In that game we must expect to be misunderstood; we must expect to misunderstand; we can try to eliminate misunderstanding but we cannot hope to completely eliminate it. One way to reduce misunderstanding is to learn and apply the ideas and formulations of general semantics.

## Suggested Activities

I. As was mentioned, strictly speaking, words don't "mean," people do. A useful method to clarify other people's meanings is to paraphrase their comments in conversations. The following is an exercise to practice this.

Pair students into dyads and give them a discussion topic (a controversial topic or topic of some complexity works best). Their purpose is to express their opinions about the topic while achieving an understanding of their partner's views.

Have one student in each of the dyads explain their views on the assigned topic to their partner. That person should paraphrase his or her understanding of those views. The first student can correct the paraphrasing if it does not accurately portray what he or she said. Allot five minutes for this part of the exercise. Then have the students reverse roles and repeat the process. At the end of the exercise ask the students these questions: What did you learn from this exercise? What are some benefits of paraphrasing? When is it especially important to paraphrase?

II. Scientists use *operational definitions* when they work on problems. These definitions describe "operations"; that is, they describe how one can know what is being referred to with words. For example: *intelligence*—a score on an IQ test; *mental disorder*—a far-reaching term that is defined more specifically in the *Diagnostic and Statistical Manual of Mental Disorders* (a medical handbook for psychiatrists); *brownies*—a recipe for making brownies would be an operational definition.

An important advantage of using operational definitions is that their specificity makes it less likely that confusion will arise over what a word means. Such confusion is fairly common in everyday life because many of the words we use are vague ones that can have a variety of meanings. Because they can have diverse meanings, vague terms can become meaningless, as the following exercise demonstrates.

Have students complete the *Instant Eloquence* exercise below. Then discuss the notion: abstract terms that lack concrete referents can confuse and deceive. (An example of this is the official name for North Korea, which is the *Democratic People's Republic of Korea*. In this "democracy" the people have no voice in their governance and human rights abuses abound. Without knowing how the DPRK "operationalizes" the term democracy one might think the DPRK is like the United States or other Western democracies that honor the principle of the free and equal right of every person to participate in their system of government.)

## Instant Eloquence

Insert the words below, in any position, in the blanks.

> *peace, justice, freedom, truth, honor, wisdom*
> What we need today is not false _____ but old-fashioned _____.
> For surely, there is no real _____ without _____. And as our
> forefathers knew so well, the price of _____ is a little _____.

III. Operational definitions can help us reach our goals. For example, if you say you want to be a rock star, "operationalize it." How would you define "rock star?" Performing at a concert for a certain number of people? Having a particular level of sales on a recording? Being signed by a label or going on tour? Once you set a concrete goal you can outline the steps it would take to get there, the operations required to meet that goal.

Discuss with the students some benefits of "operationalizing" personal goals. The following examples can be used in the discussion:

- Career counselors often help individuals by getting them to set goals, having them decide whether they are realistic and obtainable, and then assisting them to figure out the steps needed to get there.

- Rather than simply saying that one wants to become rich, setting a specific dollar amount like having a million dollars in the bank can be a spur to realizing one's desire to be wealthy.

IV. **What approach do scientists use when they work on scientific problems?** (Answer: The scientific method.) **This technique has made it possible for instant communication across continents, travel through the air, books produced by touching a button, and "wonder drugs" to cure diseases. Can you think of some other major successes that have come from the use of the scientific method?**

Present the six basic steps of the scientific method:

1. Identify a problem
2. Analyze it
3. Form a hypothesis to solve it
4. Experiment
5. Observe
6. Derive a conclusion

**Can the scientific method be used to help solve problems of everyday living—for example, problems concerning medical ailments, relationship difficulties, money management, travel, shopping, cooking, and household chores? According to the field of general semantics it can. Let's test that hypothesis.**

Ask students to identify a problem they are having and to process it through the first three steps of the scientific method. Then instruct them to design an experiment to solve the problem that can be completed within a time period less than the semester and go forward with it. Periodically review and discuss the progress that students are making on their experiments. In cases where little or no progress is being made, help students formulate a new experiment or have them alter the old one. Have individuals report to the group from time to time on how their experiments are going.

# Lesson 2:
## *Mental Maps—The Way to Better Planning and Prediction*

One look is worth one hundred reports.

—Japanese proverb

## Introduction

There is an analogy in general semantics that words and statements are like maps that describe territories. The purpose of the analogy is to remind us that words, like maps, only *represent* reality and are not reality itself: the map is not the territory.

Many people live by inaccurate maps; they have incorrect definitions or perceptions of persons, places, or things. And many people confuse their maps with the territory; they judge people and events through the labels they assign them rather than through observable actions and verifiable accounts. General semantics training emphasizes the importance of constructing accurate mental and verbal maps of persons, places, and things, and carefully restricting one's maps to most accurately convey one's meaning.

## Motivation

An accurate map, going east to west, would show New York—Chicago—Los Angeles. If the map showed New York—Los Angeles—Chicago, we would say the map was incorrect because the map was different from the actual territory. What would happen if we tried to use such a map? (Answer: We would get lost.)

Words are like mental or verbal maps. When there is a misunderstanding, conflict, or a failure in communication, it is often because our mental or verbal maps do not fit the territory—what is actually going on in the world.

## Suggested Activities

I. Let's examine some linguistic maps used in different contexts.

Discuss the following examples with the students.

- In some hotels and apartment buildings there is no floor marked 13. The elevator goes from 12 to 14 because some guests are superstitious. Is this an accurate map?

- Because of the mental maps they have formed about the horrors of middle school, some elementary school graduates do not look forward to attending middle school. When you were in elementary school how accurate were your mental maps of middle school?

- You probably have a fairly complete map for the term "average American." Think about this map for a moment. Now try to imagine the map for "average American" in the mind of the "average" Frenchman, Mexican, Russian, or Iraqi. What are some differences? How do you account for them? (This exercise can also be turned around: What is the average American's mental map of a Frenchman, Mexican, Russian, or Iraqi? Media stereotypes can also be discussed.)

- Many people are still using old maps that they developed as children and adolescents and they wonder why some things don't change for them—why they are still stuck in old thought patterns, old emotional responses, and old habits. Although your outdated maps served you well at an earlier time, they may not be effective now to achieve your desires for perhaps a higher level of health or more love or more prosperity in your life. Do you find it sometimes difficult to let go of outdated maps? Do you revise your mental maps from time to time? What do you think of the notion that even the best maps become obsolete sooner or later?

II. It is said that no two people have mental maps that are exactly similar, even for such simple words as *book*, *table*, and *house*. When we use these common terms, however, our maps are usually enough alike to prevent misunderstandings. This is not the case with many other words.

Have students write down five or ten features of their mental maps for each of the following terms.

*lawyer*

*capitalism*

*Muslim*

*President* _____ *of the U.S.*

From what materials were your mental maps constructed? (Possible responses: opinions from parents and friends, ideas from the mass media, something remembered from school or from a book.) Personal likes and dislikes frequently influence our maps. For example, Robert Potter points out in his book *Making Sense* that people who like the President will tend to judge him taller than people who dislike him.

III. The commercial production of mental maps is a multi-billion-dollar business in the United States. We call it advertising.

Advertising is an essential part of American life. Sometimes, however, the people responsible for the ads seem to know more about slick maps than about the territories (products) the maps are supposed to represent. *They stress the map, not the product.* They want us to believe that in buying the product we buy the map as well. Maps of sex appeal sell cars. Maps of social success sell deodorants. Maps of youth appeal sell cosmetic products.

Think in terms of maps (advertisements) and territories (products) as you look at the ads in a popular magazine or watch ads on TV or online. Try to find one ad that tells almost nothing about the territory and one ad that inaccurately describes the territory. Bring the ad to class or if the ad was gotten from TV or online write down your impressions of it. Be prepared to discuss the ad. (One of the issues that can be talked about when the students bring in their ads is whether the ads are offering a needed product or creating an artificial need that the product will satisfy.)

IV. Discuss with the students ways to make their mental or verbal maps more accurately fit the territories they describe. For example:

- Before making maps one should gather as much information as one can about the territory.
- Closely observe the territory before mapping it; delay your impulse to immediately produce a map about the territory.
- Understand that different maps may show different features of the same territory and that the more territory a map covers the less we can say about the territory.

# Lesson 3:
## *Extensional and Intensional Orientations—How Real Is Real?*

The universe as we know it is a joint product of the observer and the observed.

— Pierre Teilhard de Chardin, *The Phenomenon of Man*

## Introduction

In general semantics parlance, *extensionally-oriented* people are individuals who are aware that our verbal maps are never identical to the territory they represent. Such persons understand that to produce optimal map-territory congruence we must use facts, figures, measurements, descriptions, and reports from actual observations that can be verified.

*Intensionally-oriented* people tend to show more dependence on the map than on the territory. They function in a world of statements about statements, about statements, etc., on to high-level declarations. Individuals who manifest problems of adjustment tend to be highly "intensional."

A key aim of this lesson is to help people avoid the confusion that may arise as a result of not being able to discriminate between language that signifies "what is going on within one's own skin" (intensional language) and language that attempts to correspond to "what is going on out there in the 'real world' " (extensional language).

## Motivation

Hold up an inkblot picture and ask the students what they see. Typically, they will give different answers about what the picture represents. Allow this to go on until someone says, "Really, it's just a bunch of inkblots." (If no one offers that idea you should present it.) Respond by saying, "You are the only one in the group who has given what GS terms an *extensional* answer. That is, you have described the picture without projecting your own views about it."

*Extensional* responses are those that deal with what is actually going on in the world, what is outside our own skins. They can be contrasted with what GS labels *intensional* responses, reactions based on what is going on inside us, how things should be as far as we are concerned. The activities in this lesson will examine both types of responses. (Be sure to clarify the spelling of "intensional," otherwise the students will think of "intentional" responses—responses they intended.)

## Suggested Activities

I. The statements "the temperature is now ninety degrees" and "it is hot" may seem almost interchangeable, but they are not. The first statement describes an extensional condition in the world that can be objectively measured. The second statement describes the intensional nervous system reaction of a particular individual. To an Eskimo, fifty-eight degrees may be hot while to someone living in Bangkok, Thailand, fifty-eight degrees may be cold.

The distinction between extensional and intensional statements is by no means trivial. People who confuse the two types of assertions can generate arguments and misunderstandings. You cannot prove to an Eskimo that fifty-eight degrees is cool, but you *can* prove to him that it is fifty-eight degrees.

Intensional statements such as "it is hot" or "it is cool" are not a problem if the people making these statements understand that they are only expressing their opinions and that other individuals might have different takes on the matter. These statements can be a problem, however, if people making intensional statements think they are articulating objective facts. If so, they may not be willing to entertain dissent from others about those "facts."

Have you ever gotten into an argument because you or the person you were quarreling with mistook an intensional comment for an extensional one? Can you tell us about it? (Some examples of intensional comments that may provoke arguments: She's a beautiful woman. He's handsome. What a terrific movie! Great car! It's a fantastic restaurant.)

II. When we employ the word "is" to link a noun and the adjective modifying that noun (GS refers to that "is" as the *is of predication*) we can fool ourselves into thinking we are making extensional statements rather than intensional ones. For example, if we say, "John is stupid" or "Mary is smart" we imply that stupidity or smartness are characteristics of John and Mary. However, in making these declarations we are really saying more about ourselves than about John or Mary. We are *projecting* our own values, concepts, and standards of intelligence onto other people. Someone else might have different views.

In general semantics, we seek to avoid the is of predication. We have other ways to frame our sentences. For example, we might say, "John seems dim-witted to me" or "I would characterize Mary as smart." We thus acknowledge our nervous system evaluations as our own, not as existing outside our nervous system.

Have the students rephrase the following sentences to show the human element in their assertions:

- The rose is red. (Possible answer: This rose looks red to me.)
- Washington was the best president. (Possible answer: I think Washington was the best president.)
- She is rude. (Possible answer: I find her offensive.)
- They are foolish. (Possible answer: In my opinion, they are acting foolishly.)
- Teenagers are irresponsible. (Possible answer: From my vantage point, "teenagers" and "irresponsibility" are synonymous.)

III. Describe an argument you were in or one you overheard. Tell what the argument was about, who the individuals were, and what the circumstances were surrounding the fight. Indicate whether full or partial agreement was ultimately reached. Explain whether the argument was (a) due to the fact that people were unaware they were using words intensionally, or (b) due chiefly to differences in factual statements that needed more research.

IV. Professor John C. Merrill, in a chapter from his book *Journalism Ethics* titled "Korzybski to the Rescue," observes that reporters often think they are reporting or giving factual information when, in fact, they are simply expressing their own opinions. He notes:

> Journalists may use such descriptors as "an enthusiastic audience," "a beautiful painting," "impressive architecture" and the like. With these descriptions, nothing really is being said about the audience, the painting, or the architecture, there is only some clue, perhaps to the reporter's concepts of enthusiasm, beauty, and impressiveness. Such language is intensional in that we're basically learning something about the evaluative criteria of the reporter.[6]

In the coming week select a newspaper article and identify its intensional statements (observations that are not subject to verification) and extensional statements (descriptions that can be verified). Determine the proportion of intensional and extensional statements. Bring in the article and your analysis of it when we next meet.

# Lesson 4:
## *Non-Allness—No One Can Know*
## *All There Is To Know About Anything*

We see what we see because we miss all the finer details.

—Alfred Korzybski, *Science and Sanity*

## Introduction

When we notice anything in our environment we are selecting and abstracting from an infinite number of possibilities. This selection is individualistic and dependent on our nervous system, purposes, hopes, past experiences, etc. Even if we were to examine something in great detail, our knowledge of it would be incomplete because things change over time.

No word can say all about anything. A word can only reflect a personal selection of details. To remind us that there is always something left out of any description it can be useful to include a "silent etc." in our thinking when we talk about persons, things, or events.

The following ideas, which are core notions in GS philosophy, should help the students to understand that life is more a matter of dealing with probabilities than certitudes.

## Motivation

Hold up a pen or pencil and ask the students for their opinions about how long it would take to say all there is to say about the object. Then have them give descriptive statements about the item. After each statement say, "Is that *all* there is to say about the pen or pencil?" After a while it will become obvious that the group could go on indefinitely and not say *all* there is to say about the article under discussion.

We can never say all there is to know about anything. But some people say: "Oh, I know all about that." "If you know one of them, you know them all." "I know all there is to know about (fill in the blank)." People who make these kinds of statements are suffering from *allness attitudes*—they assume their mental maps tell all about the territory.

## Suggested Activities

I. Why are allness attitudes harmful? (Answer: They block communication; the person with this attitude is unable to learn and unable to change.) **What are some things you can do to rid yourself of allness attitudes?** Include the following three GS ideas for getting rid of allness attitudes in the discussion.

- Use contingent terms like *to me*, *personally*, *from where I stand*, *in my experience*, and *I think* in your speech, writing, and reflections.

- Add a "silent etc." to your thinking as a reminder that more can be said about anything.

- Adopt Alfred Korzybski's notion to *treat the familiar as unfamiliar*.

II. If we employ the word "is" (or its variants) we can say: "Liberals (Conservatives) are nincompoops." "Seeing is believing." "People with PhD's are smart." Such statements imply that *all* liberals (conservatives) are nincompoops, that seeing is *always* believing, that *all* people with PhD's are smart. However, there may be particular liberals (conservatives) who are not nincompoops, cases where seeing is deceptive, and people with PhD's who are not particularly intelligent. The use of the *is of identity* (a GS label that denotes the usage of the word "is" to link two nouns) keeps us from considering such ideas.

In general semantics we seek to avoid the is of identity by rephrasing our sentences. So, the comments cited earlier might be recast as: There are liberals (conservatives) who sometimes act like nincompoops. There are times when seeing can be believing. People with PhD's are apt to know more than other people about what they've researched.

Ask the students to come up with their own is-of-identity statements and reshape them without using the is of identity. (Some examples: "He is a genius" can be changed to "He says many clever things." "Tomatoes are vegetables" can be redone as "Tomatoes tend to be used as vegetables for culinary purposes." "Joan is a personal coach" can be restated as "Joan does personal coaching.")

III. When you have a problem that is bothering you try using plurals to talk about it. For example, in discussing your problem change the singular word "problem" to the plural word "problems." To wit, if you say, "I have a problem getting along with my boss" you may not do as much to solve it compared to saying, "I have some problems getting along with my boss." Then you might consider several problems such as:

- your constant lateness in completing assignments
- your forgetting to come to department meetings

- your never volunteering suggestions for improving productivity when your boss asks you for such feedback

Have the students provide additional examples of how one can widen their outlook by changing singulars to plurals. (Some possibilities: I'll make an effort/I'll make a number of efforts, my hope is/my hopes are, I have a method/I have several methods.)

IV. During the coming week listen for allness statements. Be prepared to discuss them and the context in which they occurred.

# Lesson 5:
## *Indexing—Getting Closer to What Is Really Going on*

Nature never rhymes her children, nor makes two men alike.

—Ralph Waldo Emerson, *Collected Essays: Second Series*

## Introduction

"No one likes me." "Sports are stupid." "If you know one Christian, Jew, Muslim, etc., you know them all." People who make remarks such as these are seeing only similarities and ignoring differences. They are deluding themselves since they probably could find exceptions to what they are saying if they gave some thought to it. They are limiting their opportunities to expand their awareness, for if one believes statements such as "no one likes me," "sports are stupid," and "if you know one Christian, Jew, Muslim, etc., you know them all," one can only react with apathy or negativism.

People who make comments like the prior ones are engaging in stereotypic thinking, a type of formulaic cognition that ignores differences and focuses on similarities. To counter such inaccurate reasoning one can use the GS technique of *indexing*, a method that involves applying index numbers to words (e.g., $car_1$, $car_2$, $car_3$, etc.) as a reminder that no two things are identical. Indexing reminds us that every person or thing is unique and has distinct characteristics.

## Motivation

No two of anything have ever been found to be identical—that is, alike in *all* respects. Can anyone come up with an example to contradict this theory? Allow students to talk about identical twins, manufactured products, etc., and have other students disprove the idea that complete identity is possible. Introduce how science can't even find total likenesses using sophisticated apparatus such as electron microscopes, etc. Yet when we speak, we talk as if things were identical. For example: "Teenagers are lazy and rude." "New Yorkers are unfriendly." "Holidays are a bore."

There is a method from mathematics to make our thinking more precise. It involves assigning subscript numbers to persons, places, or things. Thus, $teenager_1$ isn't $teenager_2$ isn't $teenager_3$, etc.; $New\ Yorker_1$ isn't $New\ Yorker_2$ isn't $New\ Yorker_3$, etc.; $holiday_1$ isn't $holiday_2$ isn't $holiday_3$, etc. GS calls this method of using numbers to make our terms and statements more descriptive, *indexing*.

## Suggested Activities

I. Present the following generalizations. After each one, have students give an example of a person, or persons, they know who defies them.

> Women are bad drivers.
>
> Men are terrible communicators.
>
> You can't teach an old dog new tricks.
>
> Blondes have more fun.

When we speak in generalities we are emphasizing likenesses and ignoring differences within groups. Indexing can help us spot those differences. To wit: woman driver$_1$ isn't woman driver$_2$ isn't woman driver$_3$, etc.; man$_1$ isn't man$_2$ isn't man$_3$, etc.; old dog$_1$ isn't old dog$_2$ isn't old dog$_3$, etc. Indexing can help us to find differences that make a difference.

II. Index numbers are usually applied to nouns. But it is also useful to apply them to verbs that can mean many things. Offer students the following examples of indexing the verb *to mean*:

- This means$_1$ trouble!  (will result in)
- Mr. Smith means$_2$ business today.  (is intent upon)
- I don't know what he means$_3$.  (wants to communicate)
- The prefix *un* means$_4$ not.  (is verbally equal to)
- Marcia means$_5$ to do very little.  (intends)

The verb *to love* can also confuse us if we fail to index. Its major meanings, in fact, are denoted by different words in some languages. How many shades of meaning can you find for your *loves*? Show that these meanings really are different by writing a separate sentence for each. Put a new index number next to *love* each time you use it with a new meaning. Also, try to write a short definition for each meaning, similar to what was done with the verb *to mean*. How many meanings can you find? Do you think it is logical to use the word *love* for all of them?

Suggested answers for this exercise:

- I love$_1$ ice cream.  (like very much)
- They loved$_2$ each other for only one night.  (shared sex)

- Oh, Tony loves$_3$ all the girls.  (is romantically attracted to)
- My parents loved$_4$ each other dearly.  (understood and selflessly respected)
- I love$_5$ my country.  (feel patriotic toward)
- Most women love$_6$ little babies.  (have a spontaneous and protective feeling for)
- I love$_7$ the Creator.  (regard with a feeling of awe and reverence)

III.  Index yourself on a given day. For example, George$_1$ the lawyer, George$_2$ the son, George$_3$ the father, George$_4$ "the drudge," George$_5$ the helper around the house. How does indexing yourself affect the way you think about yourself? Does indexing help you to see differences in yourself?

Index someone else on a given day. For example, Jill$_1$ the doctor, Jill$_2$ the mother, Jill$_3$ the friend, Jill$_4$ the flower arranger, Jill$_5$ the kick boxer. How does indexing another person affect the way you think about that person? Does indexing help you see differences in the other person?

IV.  Each of us has some prejudices, even the person who says, "My only prejudice is against prejudiced people." If you really believe you truly have no prejudices, reflect on labels such as *liberal*, *conservative*, *capitalist*, *socialist*, *politician*, *lawyer*, *opera*, *poetry*. Can you honestly say that not one of these words brought a trace of judgment to your mind?

It is not easy to conquer our prejudices even though we think we ought to. But for those willing to give it a try, the use of indexing can help. For example, New Yorker$_1$ is not New Yorker$_2$ is not New Yorker$_3$. All New Yorkers are not rude, dishonest, and immoral, even though those qualities may now be features of your stereotyped New Yorker.

In addition to indexing items, what are some other things you can do to rid yourself of prejudice? Include the following propositions in the discussion.

- To the degree you are prejudiced, you are unscientific and semantically challenged. For most individuals that is not a happy thought.
- Try to find the origins of your prejudice. For example, does the word *opera* put you off? Why? Was it because you were dragged to your first opera as a child when you really wanted to go to a rock concert?
- Try not to use labels that trigger your allness attitudes. Instead, use terms that get behind these labels. The word *poetry* can mean sonnets, light verse, limericks, haiku, Longfellow, Ginsberg, etc. The word *fish* can mean flounder, halibut, swordfish, tuna, shad, cod, etc. Say, "I've tried mackerel three times, and I don't like mackerel," not "I

hate fish."

Don't be surprised if your more serious prejudices take months or years to overcome. Remember $prejudice_1$ is not $prejudice_2$ is not $prejudice_3$.

# Lesson 6:
## *Dating—We Live in a Changing World*

One cannot step in the same river twice.

> —Heraclitus, as quoted by Plato in *Cratylus*

## Introduction

Author and business leader Robert C. Gallagher notes, "Change is inevitable—except from a vending machine."[7] On a more serious note, to remind us that change is to be expected, GS offers the technique called *dating*, a method that involves attaching dates to our evaluations. Dating can help to remind us that the world is continuously in flux, so we must be careful not to rest on our laurels when good things happen to us or become overly pessimistic in the face of adversity.

## Motivation

Since the age of the ancient Greeks we have known that "all things change, all the time"—for example: aging, rusting, fashions, clouds, etc. Can anyone deny this? Allow time for discussion.

To think more accurately about a changing world, GS recommends using a technique known as *dating*, which involves attaching dates to our evaluations. Accordingly, America$^{2015}$ is not America$^{2005}$, money exchange rates$^{\text{last year}}$ are not money exchange rates$^{\text{this year}}$, my view of the world$^{\text{today}}$ may not be my view of the world$^{\text{five years from now}}$, etc. Dating helps the map fit the territory.

## Suggested Activities

I. Dating can make a difference in the way we think about people, places, and things. For example, it would have been hard to imagine during World War II that America's most implacable enemies, Japan and Germany$^{\text{early 1940s}}$, would turn into staunch American allies, Japan and Germany$^{\text{today}}$. Similarly, rock music$^{1955}$ is not rock music$^{2015}$, computers$^{\text{five years ago}}$ are not computers$^{\text{now}}$, and you$^{\text{six months ago}}$ is not you$^{\text{at the present time}}$.

Do you think the War on Terror$^{\text{today}}$ will have the same character as the War on Terror$^{\text{ten years from now}}$? Do you think fashion designs$^{\text{this year}}$ will be the same as fashion designs$^{\text{three years hence}}$? Do you think George Bernard Shaw was on to something with respect to dating when he had a character in one of his plays say, "The only man who behaved sensibly was my tailor:

he took my measurements anew every time he saw me, whilst all the rest went on with their old measurements and expected them to fit me."[8]

II. Ten years after publishing *Teaching as a Subversive Activity,* Neil Postman published a follow-up book on education titled *Teaching as a Conserving Activity.* In the prologue to the follow-up he stated, "[M]any of the arguments which then seemed merely opposite, now seem acutely apposite, and this book is the result of a change in perspective."[9] Have you ever changed the way you viewed people or situations? What were some factors involved with that modification? Do you agree with the cliché, *when you are through changing, you are through*?

III. On a piece of paper have the students list their present age next to the current year. Instruct them to do the same for two prior four-year intervals. For example:

| Date | Age |
| ---- | --- |
| 2015 | 45 |
| 2011 | 41 |
| 2007 | 37 |

What changes were you going through during each of the time periods you listed? Review preferences in food, clothing, friends, music, sports, etc. Do you think some of your tastes today will be different four years from now? What are some benefits of "dating yourself" every now and again?

IV. Has failure to date ever led you to be surprised or into trouble? Do you always take unobserved change into account? Think of one bad experience you have had because your mental maps were not up to date. The change may have occurred in you, in another person, or in a place. Could attention to dating have helped you? If so, how?

# Lesson 7:

## *Two-Valued Orientations—The Limitations of Our "Either/or" Language*

Either you are with us, or you are with the terrorists.

—President George W. Bush, Address to Congress (Sept. 20, 2001)

## Introduction

The English language is heavily biased toward "either/or-ness," which is to say that it encourages us to talk about the world in polarities such as *hot* or *cold*, *good* or *bad*, *thin* or *fat*, *right* or *wrong*, etc. GS refers to either/or thinking as *two-valued thinking*.

Instead of framing and responding to situations using two-valued thinking, it can be beneficial to utilize what GS calls a *multi-valued approach* to reflect on the possibility of additional choices. For example, rather than narrowing down your options to going out to the movies or staying home and watching TV, a multi-valued approach allows you to brainstorm added ideas— attend a play, read a book, go out to dinner, walk around the neighborhood, etc. Having more choices typically offers a better chance at coming up with effective solutions to problems.

## Motivation

The English language often gives us convenient single words for the extremes but no words for "the great in-between." For example, one is: good or bad, happy or sad, cold or hot, right or wrong. Since we tend to classify and think with the words we know, our mental maps commonly focus on the extremes and obscure the middle. What are some problems with just concentrating on the extremes?

## Suggested Activities

I. Wouldn't it be more accurate to think in terms of "degrees" rather than "either/or extremes"? For example, where would you rate yourself on the following continuums as to how you are feeling right now?

| Cold | 1 | 2 | 3 | 4 | 5 | 6 | 7 | Hot |
|------|---|---|---|---|---|---|---|-----|
| Heavy | 1 | 2 | 3 | 4 | 5 | 6 | 7 | Light |
| Happy | 1 | 2 | 3 | 4 | 5 | 6 | 7 | Sad |

How would scientists measure the qualities listed on the aforementioned continuums? (Answer: They would quantify them by using a thermometer to measure the temperature in terms of degrees, a scale to gauge exact weight, and an attitude test to assess levels of contentment.)

What do we leave out when we use "'either/or' language"? (Answer: We leave out most of what is actually happening between the two extremes.) GS calls either/or language, *two-valued language*. Such language is exemplified in sayings such as: There are two sides to every argument. You are either with me or against me. There are only two kinds of people in this world. You're either part of the solution or part of the problem.

Can you offer further examples of two-valued assertions? How can two-valued statements restrict one's thinking about people and events?

II. Some people think about their goals in two-valued (either/or) terms. If they do not feel *successful*, they consider themselves *unsuccessful*; if not *popular*, *unpopular*; if not *happy*, *unhappy*. What are some drawbacks to thinking about one's goals in two-valued terms?

In his GS classic *People in Quandaries*, Wendell Johnson notes that people who establish two-valued goals run the risk of contracting what he labels *IFD disease*. This malady involves a person going from *I*dealization to *F*rustration to *D*emoralization due to their not attaining a goal formulated in two-valued terms. What can one do to avoid becoming a victim of IFD disease? (Some answers: embrace Alfred Korzybski's *extensional theory of happiness* [have realistic expectations, work hard, and be prepared to not get what you want]; rework unachievable goals; increase your frustration tolerance.)

III. Since human beings can think about thinking (a process GS labels *self-reflexiveness*), we can apply two-valued thinking to the subject of two-valued thinking. Thus, we can assume our thinking is *either* two-valued and not beneficial *or* multi-valued and constructive.

But this assumption is not always true. Two-valued thinking is occasionally useful. Can you give examples of such instances? (Suggested responses: A woman is either pregnant or not pregnant; many lights are wired so they must exist in one of two states: on or off; Alcoholics Anonymous insists on an intense two-valued orientation.)

IV. A *multi-valued orientation* (going beyond two-valued choices) toward the future is essential in all areas of living. It helps us to remain flexible. This doesn't always mean we have to give up our goals. It does mean, however, that we must be willing to change our goals as life changes our opportunities.

How two-valued is your approach to the future? Are you like some individuals who consider themselves failures if they finish second?

At home, write down one of your serious goals on a piece of paper (or type it on your computer). Under the goal, list three specific circumstances that might make its achievement impossible and what you think you would do in each of those situations. Be prepared to discuss your answers in class next week.

# Lesson 8:
## *Distinguishing Facts from Inferences—Language and Reality*

It is not only true that the language we use puts words in our mouths;
it also puts notions in our heads.

—Wendell Johnson, *Your Most Enchanted Listener*

## Introduction

To make accurate assessments of situations, and to avoid jumping to wrong conclusions about them, general semantics emphasizes the value of distinguishing facts from inferences. This ability is especially important when we assess ourselves. For example, thinking oneself a failure is an inference that can lead to a poor self-image that can negatively affect one's capacity to learn and perform well. Believing we are failures, we begin to act that way and so create a condition known as *a self-fulfilling prophecy*. In addition, if we strongly believe the labels we give ourselves, we may act in ways that can help to create *other-fulfilling prophecies* and have people behave toward us as if the labels we have assigned ourselves are true.

## Motivation

Read the following story to the group.

> A hunter lived with an infant in a cabin, guarded by his dog. One day the hunter returned from the fields and saw the cradle overturned and the baby nowhere in sight. The room was a mess. The dog had blood all over his muzzle. The hunter, enraged, shot the dog. He then found the baby, unharmed under the bed, and a dead wolf in the corner.

Discuss the importance of distinguishing *facts* from *inferences* using the following fact-inference taxonomy devised by Irving J. Lee.[10]

A Factual Statement

1. Can be made after some observation

2. Stays within what can be observed

3. Can be made in limited number

An Inferential Statement

1. Can be made any time

2. Goes beyond what can be observed

3. Can be made in unlimited number

| 4. Provides closest approach to certainty | 4. Shows some degree of probability |

## Suggested Activities

I. Provide the students two news stories on the same incident or event. Ask them: What facts do you find in each? What inferences? How do you evaluate the similarities and differences? What conclusions can you draw?

II. There is a cliché that says, *when you assume, you make an ass out of you and me*. But we can't not assume—it is impossible to observe, check, and test everything. The trick is to make our assumptions as accurate as possible. Presuming that to be true, reflect on an important decision you have made. What were your assumptions surrounding that decision? What additional information might you have found helpful? Was it potentially available at the time? If so, how might you have become aware of it? Were there ways to obtain that information?

III. What do you feel certain of? What makes you feel so secure in that determination? Discuss the idea that we tend to have more confidence in our inferences when they are based on observations and they converge—that is, when several inferences point to the same conclusion.

IV. In his early writings, Korzybski emphasized the idea of *logical fate*: from our assumptions, particular consequences (our conclusions, evaluations, attitudes, and behavior) inevitably follow. With this notion in mind, find someone with whom you strongly disagree about something. What assumptions do they seem to be making about the issue? If possible, ask them. Does what they say or do make sense in light of their assumptions? What assumptions do *you* make about the issue? How do these assumptions connect with your behavior?

# Lesson 9:
## *Nonverbal Communication—The Semantics of Silence*

Nonverbal communication = Ideas without words.

—Robert Potter, *Making Sense*

## Introduction

Korzybski maintained that people function within environments as *organisms-as-wholes*; that is, sensing-thinking-feeling-moving-doing forms an inseparable whole. While the notion that people behave "multi-modally" can be useful in understanding human responses in situations, Korzybski also believed there can be value in thinking about specific aspects of human responses. This lesson will concentrate on one of those aspects: nonverbal-communication.

All of us use nonverbal communication. In fact, whether we realize it or not, we engage in it most of the time. Even in the absence of words we can't help communicating. Researchers estimate that nonverbal communication (which includes wordless messages contained in body language, physical touch, facial expressions, eye contact, and voice quality) is responsible for 65-90% of all human communication.

## Motivation

Read the following story, one of Alfred Korzybski's favorites, to the students.

> A Romanian soldier, a Nazi officer, an attractive girl, and the girl's grandmother went riding together in the same compartment of a European train. Suddenly and without warning, the train plunged into a long tunnel. Total darkness: then the sound of a kiss and the resounding slap of a smack on the face. When the train pulled out of the tunnel, the Nazi's left cheek was a glowing red. What had happened? Sitting there in silence, the four persons had different thoughts. The grandmother: *What a virtuous girl my granddaughter is. I'm glad I raised her so strictly.* The girl: *Well, I'm surprised that anyone would try it, but the old lady sure knows how to defend herself.* The Nazi: *What a clever fellow these Romanians are. He kisses the girl and I get slapped for it.* And the Romanian: *How lucky I am! I kiss my own hand and get to slap a Nazi officer!*

In discussing the story, review ways to distinguish facts from inferences. Then cover the nonverbal elements in the narrative: a kiss, a slap, and a reddened cheek. Ask the students to suggest other ways people communicate without using words.

## Suggested Activities

I. Divide the students into dyads. Have each student speak to his or her partner for a few minutes. Ask the students to write down three nonverbal cues they discerned from their partner. Instruct the students to discuss how they reacted to these nonverbal cues. Ask them if they were aware of the nonverbal cues they were communicating to their partner. Talk about the idea that we sometimes project "meanings" into the "meaningless" actions of others, and they do the same with regard to us.

II. What do you intend your clothing to say about you? What does music communicate? Why do you like particular kinds of music? What effects do colors have on you? How are colors used in design? What kinds of messages do product logos convey? How far away do you stand or sit when you talk with your friends? Is it the same distance as when you speak with your boss at work? Do you communicate through touch? Why is an understanding of nonverbal communication important when interacting with people from different cultures?

III. How can *boredom* be expressed without words? (Some possible responses: yawning, resting one's head on one's hands, dozing while another person is talking.) Give some examples of other emotions and how they can be expressed nonverbally. (Some possible answers: *embarrassment*—crying, giggling, blushing; *impatience*—looking at one's watch, grimacing, fidgeting; *respect*—bowing, rising when someone enters a room, yielding a place for a person.)

IV. Korzybski invented the term *semantic reaction* to convey the idea that when people respond to things they do so in a complex manner that combines their mental, emotional, and behavioral reactions. He believed those reactions could never really be separated from one another. That is, we never react *only* verbally, *only* emotionally, or *only* physically.

Discuss the notion of semantic reactions and the multi-faceted nature of human responses.

# **Lesson 10:**
## *Signal Reactions and Symbol Reactions—Keeping Your Cool*

> Look before you leap.
>
> —Folk maxim

## **Introduction**

This lesson aims to show students the difference between a *signal reaction* (one that is instant, unthinking, and intensionally-oriented) and a *symbol reaction* (one that is delayed, mindful, and extensionally-oriented).

We easily become conditioned *signal reactors*. For example, if someone calls us a name we might quickly respond in kind or perhaps even strike out at that person. In this instance, we would be allowing words to use us rather than choosing our behaviors and reactions in a more mature manner. That latter possibility, which involves consciously delaying one's reaction in situations (GS calls it a *symbol reaction*), is emphasized in this lesson as a preferred general response.

## **Motivation**

Distribute the *Signal-Delayed Reaction Test* that appears on the next page and have the students complete it. If they haven't seen this test before most of them will probably not come up with the correct answer to it. The correct answer is 36 occurrences of the letter "f."

## Signal-Delayed Reaction Test

Directions: Go through once and count the f's.

The necessity for training farmhands for first class farms in the fatherly handling of farm livestock is foremost in the minds of farm owners. Since the forefathers of the farm owners trained the farm owners of first-class farms in the fatherly handling of farm livestock, the farm owners feel they should carry on with the family tradition of training farmhands of first-class farms in the fatherly handling of farm livestock because they believe it is the basis of good fundamental farm management.

Total number of f's ___

Review the test by pointing out the correct number of "f's" on each line.

Questions for the students:

- Did you come up with the correct answer? (Students who correctly completed the test can be complimented on carefully following instructions.)

- What kept you from getting that answer? (Some possibilities: Many people do not notice the letter "f" in the word "of" and lots of people miss counting all the "f's" because they are trying to finish the test quickly.)

- Had you taken your time and read every word carefully do you think you would have scored better on the test?

General semantics uses the terms *signal reaction* (an instant, unthinking response) and *symbol reaction* (a delayed, mindful response) to distinguish between impulsive and thoughtful reactions to situations. What are some advantages of employing symbol reactions rather than signal reactions in dealing with people and situations?

## Suggested Activities

I. Read the following anecdote to the students.

Whenever John's co-workers asked him to help them he reflexively said "yes," even if their requests concerned work not related to his job. As a result, John felt anxious and depressed much of the time from having accepted too much work. Then he decided to delay his immediate affirmative responses to his co-workers' solicitations. John mulled over which of their requests were appropriate for his involvement and which were not. As a result of doing this he turned down entreaties that he felt were out of place or he couldn't easily handle. Feeling more in control of his work conditions, John got rid of his anxiety and depression.

Review the story and discuss the proposition that it is usually a good idea to engage one's highly developed brain and nervous system (biological structures that animals farther down the evolutionary scale do not possess) to take some time to try to figure out what is going on in situations before responding to them.

II. General semantics stresses that people have power over words and their reactions to them. For example, there can be a variety of ways to reply to an insult other than a simple and automatic response. Convey this notion to the students through the following exercise.

In a role-play, have one student call another "an idiot." Instruct the student called the name to write it down on a piece of paper and carefully think about the word. **Does being called an idiot really make one an idiot? Can a mere word magically change someone into something a person is not? How smart is it to let another individual control your reactions when being called a name?** Discuss the idea that delaying one's reactions can help one to not impulsively react to words. Talk about the thought that putting someone down and calling him or her a name can narrow the way one thinks about that person and can cause one to overlook his or her positive attributes.

III. Neil Postman, the author of a GS-related book titled *Crazy Talk, Stupid Talk*, notes that slogans are a type of propaganda that is intended to go beyond our reasoning and penetrate to places where our emotions are stored.[11] What they hope to elicit is a signal reaction. Some examples of slogans include: "On, Wisconsin!" "Let's go, Mets!" "Sieg heil" and "Deutschland über alles." Have students come up with some other slogans that elicit signal reactions.

Sloganeering involves a negation of individual thought. It is practiced in many ways—in pledges, oaths, banners, bumper stickers, college cheers, mantras—whenever it appears desirable to ease the burden of individual responsibility for thinking a matter through. Knowing this, Postman says when you're in a crowd you may want to applaud, cheer, or chant anyway on the grounds that it is good for you to "let go." Or you may feel the need to submerge yourself in a collectivized mood. But he warns that unless there is some part of you that knows exactly what is happening and that has retained the option to withdraw, there can be a danger you will be drawn into a multitude that has lost its power of reasoning and moral choice. (Aldous Huxley in *Brave New World* gave a name to this danger: *herd poisoning.*)

Do you think about slogans and their intended uses before responding to them? Why do you think slogans are often effective in mobilizing people toward particular goals? Do you think schools should educate more on the uses and misuses of propaganda?

IV. Think about a time when you got angry. What did you tell yourself that brought on the anger? (Standard responses typically include statements that include the words *should, I can't stand it,* or *how dare they*. To wit: "They shouldn't have behaved that way." "I can't stand it when they act like that." "How dare they conduct themselves in that manner!")

Albert Ellis, the founder of Rational-Emotive Behavior Therapy, a school of psychology that makes use of many GS formulations, maintains if people change what they tell themselves they won't get angry in the first place.[12] For example, instead of instantly reverting to "should," "can't stand it," or "how dare they" thoughts in "anger-producing" situations, Ellis suggests taking some time to think about what is going on and substituting statements of preference: "I would prefer they didn't behave this way." "I don't like the way they are acting, and wish they would behave differently, but I can stand it." "I would be happier if people reacted the way I wanted them to, but I don't control the universe." Such substitutions can help one to feel less angry and consequently be more likely to say and do things to improve the upsetting situation one is in—or at least not make the situation worse.

Do you think following Ellis's advice on how to not get angry would work for you? One way to find out is to try it in the coming week and report back on what happened.

# Lesson 11:
## *Increasing Semantic Awareness*
## *—The Structural Differential*

A preacher, professor, journalist, or politician whose high-level abstractions can systematically and surely be referred to lower level abstractions is not only talking, he is saying something.

—S. I. Hayakawa, *Language in Thought and Action*

## Introduction

There is a natural order of abstracting that begins with sensation and then proceeds to verbal levels. Such levels consist of names (the naming level), descriptions (the descriptive level), and then inferences, opinions, assumptions, judgments, generalizations, theories, laws, etc.

A basic goal of general semantics is consciousness of the natural order of abstraction as well as the *process* of abstracting—a process of neurological steps by which we take in information from our environment: first, events *happen*, then we *sense* those events, then we *describe* those events, then we make *inferences* about those events. The *structural differential* (a GS tool that shows how the abstracting process works) can help us to understand the process of abstracting.

## Motivation

To modern science there is no solid matter. If matter looks solid to us it does so only because its motion is too rapid or too minute to be felt. We perceive such matter with our senses but cannot say all about it with words because matter is constantly changing, sometimes slowly, sometimes quickly. As a result, whenever we communicate with words we always leave things out. The process of taking in the material world and formulating our observations of it into words is referred to as *abstracting*.

General semantics offers a diagrammatic way of understanding the abstracting process (a process that involves events that happen; how we sense those events; how we describe those events; and how we make inferences about those events) through a graphic model known as the *structural differential*.

The structural differential was designed to give an idea of how the abstracting process works and to show that the more abstract our language, the fewer characteristics it describes. To illustrate the workings of the structural differential let's use the example of Bowser, a cocker spaniel dog. Distribute the structural differential diagram that appears on the next page and have the students refer to it as you go through the numbered steps on pages 43 and 44 that explain how it functions. (NB: Step 1 in the numbered explanation refers to the broken parabola at the top of the diagram. Step 2 refers to the circle below the parabola. The rest of the steps refer to the "tags" that appear below the circle. Tell the students that Steps 6 and 7 [$L_3$ and $L_4$] are not included in the diagram due to space considerations.)

It is recommended that a display model of the structural differential be used in teaching this lesson. The Institute of General Semantics sells such models at:

www.generalsemantics.org/store/teaching-aids/80-the-structural-differential-vinyl-wall-hanging.html

# The Structural Differential

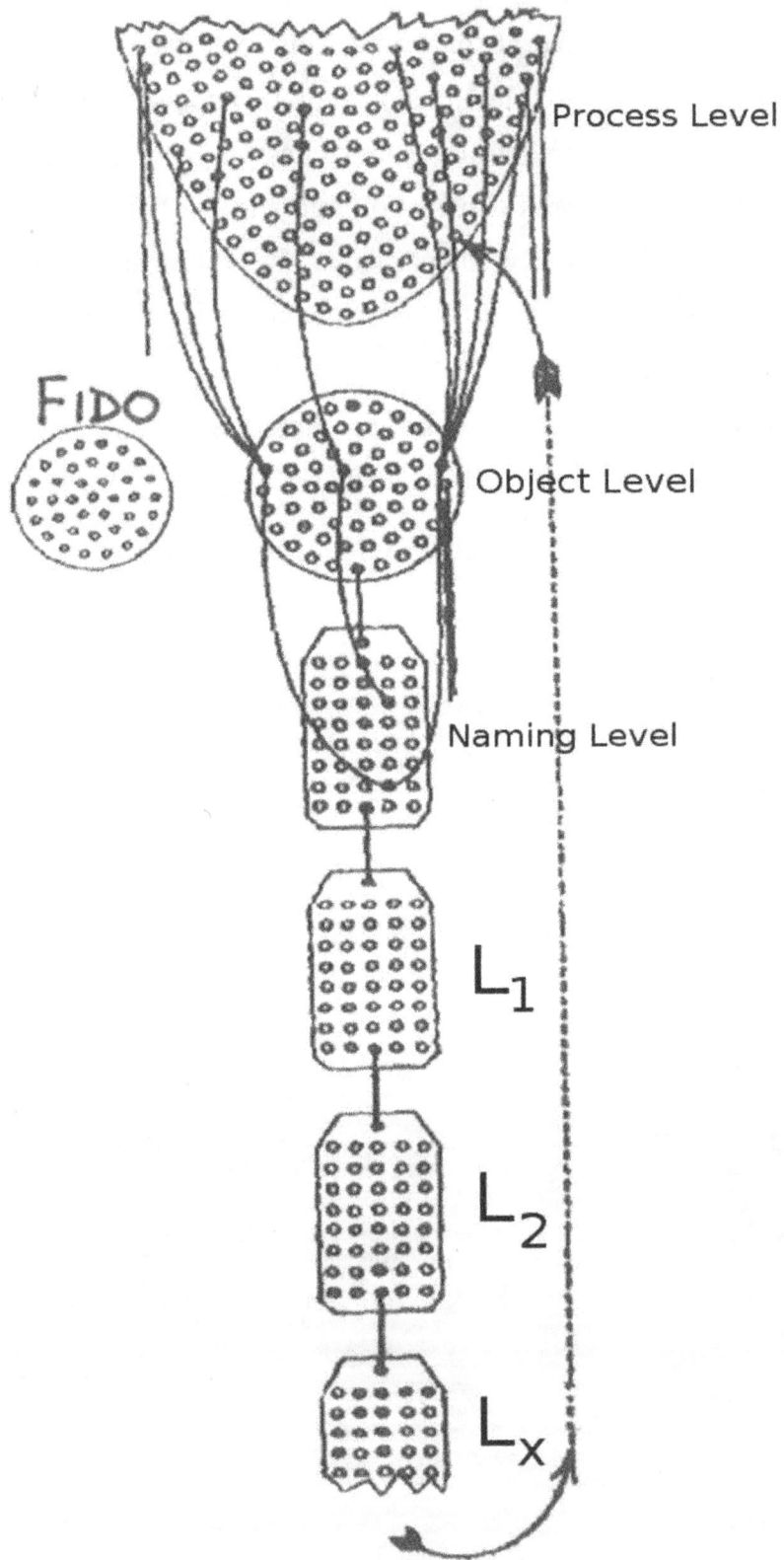

### *The workings of the structural differential explained through the example of "Bowser, a cocker spaniel dog"*

1.  The *process level* (represented by the broken parabola): Dogs, and all other objects in the world, ultimately consist of atoms, electrons, and other minute particles we cannot detect through normal human senses. Characteristics (represented by circles) are infinite at this level and ever changing.

2.  The *object level* (represented by the circle under the parabola): The dog we perceive is not the word, but the object of experience, that which our nervous system selects (abstracts) from the totality that constitutes the process-dog. Many of the characteristics of the process-dog are left out. This is the *object* or macroscopic level of "sense data," somewhat different for each person and from one time to another. The *FIDO* (animal) circle indicates that animals also abstract at the object level. However, an animal's capacity to make inferences or related associations is finite, unlike a human's. There are no attachments to verbal levels because for an animal the object as perceived is all there is. Unlike people, animals cannot symbolize their experiences through words.

3.  The *naming level*: The word "Bowser" is the *name* we give to the object of perception at the third level of abstraction. The name *is not* the object; it merely *stands* for the object and omits references to many of the characteristics of the object. Please note, the connecting strings indicate the characteristics that are included in the subsequent level. As we abstract, or select, we include fewer and fewer of the originally perceived characteristics and introduce new characteristics by implication.

4.  $L_1$ (the label or descriptive level): We can make a statement about our dog: "Bowser is a cocker spaniel." Again characteristics are left out, as the broad term "cocker spaniel" has fewer characteristics associated with it than the animal we have labeled "Bowser." Under "cocker spaniels," we can include features that Bowser shares with other cocker spaniels.

5.  $L_2$: At this level we might say: "Cocker spaniels are dogs." Once more we are leaving out characteristics, as "cocker spaniels" and "dogs" are broad categories that are vaguely descriptive of specific animals within those categories.

6.  $L_3$ (not shown on the diagram due to space considerations): At this level we are far enough from Bowser himself to introduce inferences and value judgments. So, after

observing Bowser hurriedly devouring his supper we might conclude: "Dogs eat quickly." That statement is farther from "reality" than the $L_1$ comment: "Bowser is a cocker spaniel."

7. $L_4$ (not shown on the diagram due to space considerations): After seeing that Bowser runs up to us when we come home and licks our face and wags his tail, we might make the inference that dogs are good animals. This remark relates not to dogs per se, but to our feelings about dogs. We might be closer to the "truth" about dogs if we said instead: "I like dogs."

8. $L_x$: The circular line from $L_x$ to the process level is meant to show that although inferences are the last step in the abstracting process, we must always start with something inferred.

## Suggested Activities

I. The purpose of the structural differential is to help people understand a number of patterns and relationships. First, we have the relationship between atomic "reality" and the "things" we see. Next, comes the relationship between these things and the labels we give them. Finally, there are the many relationships between labels on purely verbal levels. Do you think the structural differential accomplishes its purposes well? If not, what additions or simplifications would you propose. (A possible suggestion: Some people have been confused by having to look *down* the structural differential to reach *high* levels of abstraction. They would like to see the model inverted.)

II. High-level abstractions do not refer to "things" in reality, although they seem to. For example, in his *Lecture Notes on Teaching General Semantics*, Professor Lance Strate observes: "[W]e talk about nations as if they were real things, but there is no agreement on how to define *nation* or what constitutes a nation, no objective tests to determine whether some entity is a nation."[13] What are some other examples of high-level abstractions that seem to reflect "actual" things, but do not? Some possible answers:

- the id, ego, and superego
- the mind
- a person's race (the definition of race differs from one culture to another—in the U.S. we have traditionally defined white vs. black on an all-or-nothing basis of purity, other cultures in the western hemisphere have at least one category of mulatto)
- intelligence (because the word exists we assume that the thing it refers to exists and we try to

find it, describe it, measure it, test it)

III. We live in a process world. But our language does not accurately reflect this fact because it allows us to "split" into separate words what cannot be split in "the real world." For example, we talk about the *mind* and the *body* as if they were separate entities. But that is not correct. Can there be a mind without a body? Lacking a body, there would be no mind. And without the mind, what would the body be? Moreover, the chemical processes of the body affect the mind—that's why antidepressants work. And the opposite is true. Our mental state can influence our physical condition—worry can aggravate ulcers and other bodily ailments.

General semantics calls this tendency to use isolating words *elementalism.* We practice elementalism when we let the word *flower* make us forget that the "real" flower is an ever-changing process that requires air, light, water, and soil. When we put a flower into words we should not fool ourselves into thinking we are fully describing a real flower. The structural differential shows that "reality" is far too complex to be subsumed by a single label.

Elementalism is firmly established in our language and when we use words its effects cannot easily be avoided. But there are GS ideas that can mitigate its power. For example, we can put quotes around elementalistic terminology. We can also use hyphens to link words that are not, by themselves, descriptions of "reality." Albert Einstein, recognizing the oneness of space and time, created the notion of space-time. Can you think of other words that might be linked together to lessen their elementalistic effects? (Some possible answers: psycho-biological, neuro-linguistic, socio-cognitive, etc.)

IV. Some of our most important words (such as *love, hate, prejudice, truth, cause, effect*) can be assigned definite meanings only when we specify the level of abstraction at which they function. For example, do you love someone? Do you love loving them? Do you love loving love? Do you have a prejudice against prejudice? Are there facts you can learn about facts? Can you feel anxious about your anxiety? GS labels words that can function on diverse levels *multiordinal.*

What are some other examples of multiordinal terms? (Some possible answers: *fear, fault, reality, structure,* and *existence.*) Why can it be useful to define multiordinal terms clearly? (Some possible answers: If someone says they love and want to marry you, it is probably a good idea to know with some specificity their meaning of the word "love"; one way to not waste time arguing with someone over the "truth" of something is to have both parties state how they are characterizing truth and how they would know it; the reality of a situation can vary depending on who is defining the term "reality" and what their purposes are in the circumstances in which that word is being defined.)

# Lesson 12:

## *Asking Constructive Questions—Ones that Show an Extensional Orientation*

There cannot be a precise answer to a vague question.

—Wendell Johnson, *People in Quandaries*

## Introduction

General semantics encourages the asking of "constructive questions" that can help us to make extensional observations and take meaningful actions. When people do not know how to ask constructive questions, problems may arise:

1. Individuals may address a particular issue by simply worrying about it. For example:

    a.    Teacher: How can I teach such a large class? Do these students know as much as students did twenty-five years ago?

    b.    Student: How can I show this poor report card to my parents? Why do I have to go to school?"

2. People may think they can solve their problems if they just find the right book, or take the proper courses, or find a dependable adviser to answer their questions—that one right answer must be somewhere.

The following lesson focuses on ways to ask constructive questions.

## Motivation

Sometimes we waste time trying to answer questions that are useless, contradictory, or unanswerable. For example: Which came first, the egg or the chicken? Can you square a circle?

These are extreme cases of contradictory statements that can be argued either way without reaching any valid result. Can you come up with similar questions? What are some adjectives that can describe these questions? (Possible answers: nonsensical, useless, unanswerable, etc.) GS classifies such questions as *unsane*.

## Suggested Activities

I. Change each of the following *unsane* questions into constructive ones (questions whose solutions lead to useful observations or taking positive action).

- Unsane question: Why couldn't I have been born rich, smart, happy, etc.?

Constructive question: _____?

(A possible response: What can I do right now to become more wealthy, intelligent, content, etc.?)

- Unsane question: Will I ever be a success?

Constructive question: _____?

(A possible response: What's the best way to prepare for my job interview?)

- Unsane question: Can I ever be happy?

Constructive question: _____?

(A possible response: Is there a place around here where I can buy a cup of coffee and a doughnut?)

- Unsane question: Why are people so unkind?

Constructive question: _____?

(A possible response: Why didn't you wait for me?)

- Unsane question: Why did this have to happen to me?

Constructive question: _____?

(A possible response: How can I change this unfortunate situation?)

Have each student devise an unsane question and transform it into a constructive one.

When you changed your unsane question into a constructive one it provided you with a way to move forward. You could either answer your question or act on it.

What effect does asking unsane questions have on the people who do the asking? (Answer: They keep such individuals in quandaries.)

What effect do unsane questions have on people who attempt to answer them? (Answer: Unsane questions can lead these people to feel anxious, angry, or confused.)

II. The ways questions are asked set the terminology and structure of their answers. For example, the question "what is *the* way to do x," may elicit the response "the way to do x is this way" (which implies that there are no other ways to do x). And the question "am I a good person or a bad person," may produce the reply "of course, you're a good person" (which suggests that the question you asked was a reasonable one that could *only* be answered in two possible ways).

As children, when the teacher asked us questions in the classroom, many of us were conditioned to search for answers. Do you think a case can be made that a better education would have had us first think about the questions? Why do you think schools have neglected the study of question asking? Do you think it would make sense to include the art of question asking as an essential component in the field of language education?

III. Consider the question: Why does everyone constantly pick on me? This is an unsane inquiry because where and how would we find an answer to it? We need to know what the person means by "everyone" and "constantly." And even with these words defined, how would we determine the motivations of each individual involved? In this instance, some constructive questions to ask might be: "Today, who picked on me?" "Who left me alone?" "How can I find out why I am being picked on?" In what ways do these questions show an extensional orientation? (Answer: They involve indexing, dating, and focusing on details. They deal with non-allness, since we are no longer putting everyone into a single category. They are questions designed to elicit concrete answers.)

IV. In journalism, the *Five W's* (also known as the *Five W's and one H,* or *Six W's*) is a concept in news research and police investigations that is regarded as basic to information gathering. It is a formula for getting the full story on something. The key idea of the *Five W's* is that for a report to be considered complete it must answer a checklist of six constructive questions, each of which comprises an interrogative word:

- *Who* is it about?
- *What* happened?
- *When* did it take place?
- *Where* did it occur?
- *Why* did it happen?
- *How* did it happen?

The next time you are somewhere interesting, pause and ask yourself the Five W's: who, what, when, where, why, and how? Consider it an exercise—you're stretching your brain to nurture a journalistic mindset. And if you happen to find an actual story in the process, great!

# Notes

1. A list of some of the many different fields GS has influenced, with specifics detailing that influence, can be found at Martin H. Levinson, "General Semantics And . . .," *ETC: A Review of General Semantics* 67 no. 2 (April 2010): 127-143.

2. This Teacher's Guide was put together by Institute of General Semantics President Martin H. Levinson, with editorial assistance from IGS Trustee and Webmaster Ben Hauck. Some activities included in it originally appeared in or were adapted from Susan Presby Kodish and Bruce I. Kodish, *Drive Yourself Sane*. 3rd ed. rev. (Pasadena, CA: Extensional Publishing, 2010), a superb introduction to general semantics; S.I. Hayakawa, *Language in Thought and Action* (New York: Harcourt Brace, 1990), a GS classic on the role of language in human life; Robert Potter, *Making Sense* (New York: Globe, 1974), a high school/college text on general semantics and critical thinking; and Catherine Minteer, *Words and What They Do to You* (Fort Worth, TX: Institute of General Semantics, 2004), a GS primer directed toward middle- and high-school students.

3. Irving J. Lee, "On Language and General Semantics," *General Semantics Bulletin* 22-23 (1958): 59.

4. Kenneth G. Johnson, *General Semantics: An Outline Survey,* 3rd ed. rev. (Fort Worth, TX: Institute of General Semantics, 2004), 21.

5. Ibid., 21.

6. John C. Merrill, *Journalism Ethics: Philosophical Foundations for News Media* (New York: St. Martin's, 1996), 166.

7. Gyles Brandreth, *Oxford Dictionary of Humorous Quotations,* 5th ed.(Oxford: Oxford University Press, 2013), 212.

8. George Bernard Shaw, "Man and Superman," in *Man and Superman and Three Other Plays* (New York: Barnes and Noble Classics, 2004), 368.

9. Neil Postman, *Teaching as a Conserving Activity* (New York: Delacorte, 1979), 2.

10. Johnson, *General Semantics: An Outline Survey*, 13.

11. Neil Postman, *Crazy Talk, Stupid Talk* (New York: Delacorte, 1976), 195.

12. Albert Ellis, *How to Stubbornly Refulse to Make Yourself Miserable About Anything—Yes Anything!* (New York: Lyle Stuart, 1995), 47.

13. Lance Strate, "Lance Strate's Lecture Notes on Teaching General Semantics," *generalsemantics.org,* Retrieved Sep 08 2014 from http://www.generalsemantics.org/wp-content/uploads/2011/04/lecture-notes-on-teaching-general-semantics-by-lance-strate.pdf

# A Brief Annotated Bibliography

Hayakawa, S. I. *Language in Thought and Action*. 5th ed. New York: Harcourt Brace, 1990.

> This book discusses the role of language in human life, the many functions of language, and how language sometimes without our knowing—shapes our thinking.

Johnson, Kenneth G. *General Semantics: An Outline Survey*. 3rd ed. rev. Concord, CA: Institute of General Semantics, 2004.

> This thoughtfully organized outline survey provides a concise summary of general semantics, a cross-referenced index of key topics, and a six-page bibliography.

Johnson, Wendell. *People in Quandaries: The Semantics of Personal Adjustment*. Concord, CA: International Society for General Semantics, 2002.

> One of the most popular college texts in general semantics, *PIQ* deals with the "mechanics" of disappointments, frustrations, and other sources of unhappiness. Included in it are analyses of the role language plays in creating maladjustment and applications of the scientific method useful in daily life.

Kodish, Susan Presby, and Bruce I. Kodish. *Drive Yourself Sane: Using the Uncommon Sense of General Semantics*. 3rd ed. rev. Pasadena, CA: Extensional Publishing, 2010.

> This book contains general semantics applications, exercises, a glossary of general semantics terms, a short biography of Alfred Korzybski, and a foreword by Alfred Ellis describing the benefits of general semantics to productive living.

Korzybski, Alfred. *Selections from Science and Sanity*. 2nd ed. Edited by Lance Strate. Fort Worth, TX: Institute of General Semantics, 2010.

> This volume represents Alfred Korzybski's authorized abridgement of his magnum opus, *Science and Sanity: An Introduction to Non-Aristotelian Systems and General Semantics*. The second edition contains new introductory material and a revised index, providing an accessible introduction to Korzybski's arguments concerning the need for a non-Aristotelian approach to knowledge, thought, perception, and language.

Levinson, Martin H. *Sensible Thinking for Turbulent Times*. Lincoln, NE: iUniverse, 2006.

> This book, which is based on GS ideas and formulations, offers practical ways to improve one's thinking ability, emotional self-management, creativity, and analysis of important social issues.

Levinson, Martin H. *Practical Fairy Tales for Everyday Living*. Lincoln, NE: iUniverse, 2007.

This collection of twenty-five fanciful stories features characters who successfully battle a variety of personal problems and mishaps using notions gleaned from general semantics.

Postman, Neil. *Crazy Talk, Stupid Talk*. New York: Delacorte, 1976.

Employing a variety of GS formulations, the author identifies and explains how we defeat ourselves by the way we talk, and what we can do about it.

www.ingramcontent.com/pod-product-compliance
Lightning Source LLC
Chambersburg PA
CBHW080938040426

42443CB00015B/3461

9 780986 076497